CD INCLUDES  54 TRACKS!

WORLD BEAT RHYTHMS
BEYOND THE DRUM CIRCLE
USA

For Drummers, Percussionists, Music Therapists, Band Directors, and All Musicians

by Maria Martinez & Ed Roscetti

Cover photo by Matthew Fried

ISBN 978-1-4234-4126-7

HAL•LEONARD®
CORPORATION

7777 W. BLUEMOUND RD. P.O. BOX 13819 MILWAUKEE, WI 53213

In Australia Contact:
Hal Leonard Australia Pty. Ltd.
4 Lentara Court
Cheltenham, Victoria, 3192 Australia
Email: ausadmin@halleonard.com.au

Visit Hal Leonard Online at
www.halleonard.com

Foreword

Ed Roscetti and Maria Martinez have come up with a truly unique concept, bringing together educators, students, professionals, music therapists, and hobbyists of all ages with their *World Beat Rhythms Beyond the Drum Circle* book/CD series. The books are easy to follow and each chapter is self-contained with instrument photos, rhythm indexes, grooves, and percussion scores. They make the learning process fun and enjoyable. Ed and Maria's approach helps to increase your rhythmic vocabulary, develop authenticity, and open the door for your own musical creativity. It's appropriate for musicians of all levels who play any instrument, as well as drummers and percussionists. This book/CD series is a great asset to all music educators and band directors to get their orchestras, band ensembles, and students of all ages groovin' together. I highly recommend the *World Beat Rhythms (WBR) Beyond the Drum Circle* series.

—Joe Porcaro

About the Authors

MARIA MARTINEZ, originally from Camaguey, Cuba and raised in New Orleans, Louisiana, is a respected drummer, percussionist, clinician, and educator, now living and working in Los Angeles since 1981. She is the author of several educational publications, including *Rudimental Warm-Ups* (book/CD package), *Instant Guide to Drum Grooves* (book/CD package), *Brazilian Coordination for Drumset*, and *Afro-Cuban Coordination for Drumset* (DVD, video, and book/CD packages), all published by Hal Leonard.

Maria has contributed published articles for *Modern Drummer Magazine*, *Percussive Notes*, *Drum Magazine*, *Latin Percussion Educational Newsletter*, and *Drum Instructors Only Newsletter*. She is co-founder and author of the "World Beat Rhythms (WBR) Beyond the Drum Circle" Workshop Series and the *WBR Beyond the Drum Circle* book/CD series, including *WBR-Brazil*, *WBR-Africa*, *WBR-Cuba*, and *WBR-USA* (Hal Leonard). She has taught master classes, conducted clinics, and played at events such as PASIC (Percussive Arts Society International Convention), NAMM (National American Music Merchants), and TCAP (The California Arts Project), among others.

Martinez pursues an active freelance career, having performed and shared both stage and studio with such artists as Angela Bofill, Klymaxx, Morris Albert, El Chicano, Rita Coolidge, Emmanuel, Trini Lopez, Lisa Haley and the Zydekats, the late Barry White, Nel Carter, and Johnny Paycheck. Her television and recording appearances include *The Late Show*, *The Drew Carey Show*, *Dukes of Hazzard*, *No Borders* (CD), *Soul Train*, *Desde Hollywood* (Univision), and others.

Maria endorses Drum Workshop/Pacific, Paiste, Regal Tip, Latin Percussion, Remo Heads, E-Pad Company, Rhythm Tech, Factory Metal Percussion, and D'Addario/Pure Sound.

Professional Affiliations:
American Society of Composers, Authors and Publishers (ASCAP)
American Federation of Musicians (AFM)
Percussive Arts Society (PAS)

ED ROSCETTI is a drummer, composer, educator, author, and clinician. Roscetti has performed, produced and composed for numerous records, TV shows, and films including *Mostly Ghostly*, *Saturday Night Live*, *The 60's*, *The Secret*, *Famous*, The History Channel, WWE, *Property Ladder*, *General Hospital*, and *Santa Barbara*. He has also worked or collaborated with Quincy Jones, Herbie Hancock, Joe Sample, and the Crusaders, among others.

His critically-praised Hal Leonard book/CD packages include, *Drummers Guide to Odd Meters*, *Blues Drumming*, *Funk & Hip Hop Drumming*, *Rock Drumming Workbook*, *Stuff! Good Drummers Should Know*, and *Creating Professional Drum Loops* (Music Sales Group). He is co-founder of the "World Beat Rhythms (WBR) Beyond the Drum Circle" Workshop Series and the *WBR Beyond the Drum Circle* book/CD series, including *WBR-Brazil*, *WBR-Africa*, *WBR-Cuba,* and *WBR-USA* (Hal Leonard). He has been a core curriculum author for 28 years at Musician's Institute (PIT) and conducts concerts, clinics, workshops, and music camps across the country. He is currently working on numerous composing and production projects. See the events/news page at roscettimusic. com for current project updates.

Ed endorses Drum Workshop/Pacific, Gon Bops, Paiste, Remo, Regal Tip, Shure Inc., D'Addario/Puresound, E-Pad, and Factory Metal Percussion.

Professional Affiliations:
American Society of Composers, Authors and Publishers (ASCAP)
National Association of Recording Arts and Sciences (NARAS)
American Federation of Musicians (AFM)
Society of Composers and Lyricists (SCL)
Percussive Arts Society (PAS)

Dedication

We would like to dedicate this book to all the sponsors of World Beat Rhythms.

Special Thanks to:
Robin Wright, Claudia Dunn, Joe Porcaro, Steve & Stefanie Hilstein, Joanna Downey, the late Bill Miller, Carolyn Grant, Jillian Jepsen, Eric Ebel, Tina Wilson, Howard Emmons, Leo Adamian, Jeff Simons, Ryan & Leah Stohs, Chris Trujillo, Rick Mattingly, Steve Venz, Yoav DeBasc, Damon Tedesco, Sebastian Aymanns, Fred Engler, David Hughes, Corey Flanigan, Jeff Stern, Rich Mangicaro, Louie Marino, Groovetoons Publishing, Roscetti Music, Doug Lady, Jeff Schroedl, Bruce Bush, C.G. Ryche, Eric Dawson, Ryan Poyer, and everyone at Hal Leonard.

Thanks for Your Support:
Scott Donnell, Juels Thomas, Nikki Paredes, Garrison, Steven Vega, John Good, Don Lombardi, and Andrew Meskin (Drum Workshop/Pacific) (Gon Bops)
Erik & Kelly Paiste, Ed Clift, Tim Shahady, Wayne Wilburn, Andrew Shreve, and Lori Armenta (Paiste)
Carol Calato, Cathy Calato, Lori Penque, and Jason Medynski (Regal Tip)
Brock Kaericher, Bruce Jacoby, Michelle Jacoby, Mike DeMenno, Jerry Zacarias, Eduardo Chalo, Matt Connors, and Chris Hart (Remo)
Steve Nigohosian, Angelo Arimborgo, Memo Acevedo, Terry Tlatelpa, Kimberly Redl, Lori Hagopian, David McAllister, Heidi Schaeffer, Kim Graham, and Martin Cohen (Latin Percussion)
Ed Eblen and Lynn Rutherford (E-Pad Company)
Jim Bailey, Hugh Gilmartin, and Michael Robinson (D'Addario/Puresound)
Jim Andersen (Factory Metal Percussion)
Steve Westphal (Vaughncraft Percussion)
Ryan Smith (Shure, Inc.)
Dean Bowder (Protection Racket)

WBR Uses the Following Equipment and Software:
Pacific Platinum Exotic and LX Series Drumset (Drum Workshop/Pacific) www.pacificdrums.com
DW Pedals and Hardware (DW) www.dwdrums.com
Paiste Cymbals & Gongs (Paiste) www.paiste.com
Remo Drum Heads and World Percussion (Remo) www.remo.com
LP Congas, Udu Drums and misc. hand percussion (Latin Percussion) www.lpmusic.com
Celtic Bells and Cross Crasherz (Factory Metal Percussion) www.factorymetalpercussion.com
Pure Sound Snare Wires (D'Addario/Puresound) www.daddario.com
Shaker (Canz) (Rhythm Tech) www.rhythmtech.com
Sticks, Brushes, and Mallets (Regal Tip) www.regaltip.com
KSM 44's, KSM 32's, KSM 27's, and Beta Series Microphones (Shure, Inc.) www.shure.com
20/20 Biamplified Studio Monitors & 5.1 Surround (Event Electronics) www.event1.com
Protools HD & LE (003) (DigiDesign) www.digidesign.com
Digimax Mic Pre (Presonus) www.presonus.com

All percussion scores composed, arranged and produced by Ed Roscetti and Maria Martinez, Groovetoons (ASCAP) and Sugar Cube (ASCAP) © 2008 All Rights Reserved

Drums and Percussion:	Maria Martinez and Ed Roscetti
Bass:	David Hughes
Piano:	Steve Donovan
Bass and Piano Arrangements:	Ed Roscetti

Recorded at Roscetti Music, Studio City, California by Ed Roscetti, Fred Engler, and Silvio Bruno
Mixed at Roscetti Music, Studio City, California by Ed Roscetti

DAW & Studio:	Fred Engler
CD Mastering:	Damon Tedesco
Drum Tech/Cartage:	Sebastian Aymanns
Photographer:	Larry Plumeri
Photographer Cover and Chapter:	Matthew Fried

Table of Contents

Introduction

World Beat Rhythms (WBR) Beyond the Drum Circle-USA is part of a book/CD series that explores rhythmic styles from different regions of the world. The hybrid compositions and rhythms in this book are influenced by the popular blues, jazz, Bo Diddley, second line, rock, and hip hop styles of the United States.

In this workbook you will learn hybrid rhythms on drumset and different percussion instruments. Both traditional and non-traditional instruments were used to play the compositions, and we encourage you to use an alternate for any instrument you may not own. This hands-on approach will teach musicians and non-musicians of all levels how to feel and move time with each percussion part, while gaining a rhythmic awareness that can be applied to any musical instrument.

Specifically, the book contains photographs of each percussion instrument, instruction on techniques used to play each instrument, rhythm indexes, worksheets, percussion scores, percussion breaks, charts, and audio examples of each rhythm demonstrated on their respective instruments. Each chapter is self-contained, and in addition you will be able to play along with the entire percussion ensemble (accompanied by bass guitar) on the CD, recorded with and without a drumset.

The "World Beat Rhythms Beyond the Drum Circle" series includes *WBR-Brazil*, *WBR-Africa*, *WBR-Cuba*, and *WBR-USA*. It's an invaluable tool for all students from beginners to advanced levels and music educators and/or music therapists who are teaching students to have a deeper awareness of time and time-feel. This material can be used for teaching groups or a single student. In addition to using this book/CD package, we encourage you to play with other people and have a good time.

About the Recording

In order to assist you in developing the proper "feel" for the rhythms covered in this book, the accompanying compact disc features demonstration and play-along tracks that can be used when learning and practicing the examples. The demonstrations on the CD are identified with the corresponding track number under an icon next to the written example.

CD Track Log

This log lists the specific instruments heard on each track on the accompanying CD.

Chapter 1: Blues/Jazz
1) Rhythm Index (quarter note equals 87)
2) Click, Drumset (Intro, A Sections)
3) Click, Tambourine (Intro, A Sections)
4) Click, Tubano (Intro, A Sections)
5) Click, Drumset (B Sections)
6) Click, Tambourine (B Sections)
7) Click, Conga and Tumbadora (B Sections)
8) Click, Bass Drum 2 (Percussion Break)
9) Click, Gankogui Bell (Percussion Break)
10) Click, Shekere (Percussion Break)
11) Click, Large Bata (Percussion Break)
12) Click, Medium Bata (Percussion Break)
13) Click, Small Bata (Percussion Break)
14) Click, Handbourine and Shaker (Percussion Break)
15) Click, Caxixi (Percussion Break Section C2)
16) Click, Drumset (D Section)
17) Click, Drumset (E Section, double time)
18) Click, Unison Ending (refer to chart)
19) Chart with Drumset
20) Chart without Drumset

Chapter 2: Bo Diddley/Second Line/Rock
21) Rhythm Index (quarter note equals 75)
22) Click, Clay/Udu Drums (Intro, Interlude)
23) Click, Djun-Djun (Intro, Interlude)
24) Click, Tambourine (A Sections)
25) Click, Rainstick (A Sections)

26) Click, Drumset (A Sections)
27) Click, Snare Drum, Surdo (Break 1)
28) Click, Doumbek, Bongo (Break 1)
29) Click, Metal Guiro, Ago-sha (Break 1)
30) Click, Remo Gong Drum (Break 1)
31) Click, Suspended Cymbal (Break 1)
32) Click, Drumset (B Sections)
33) Click, Tambourine (B Sections)
34) Click, Conga Tumbadora (B Sections)
35) Click, Doumbek (B Sections)
36) Click, Surdo (B Sections)
37) Click, Drumset Bo Diddley Breakdown (B Sections)
38) Click, Taiko Drums (B Sections)
39) Chart with Drumset
40) Chart without Drumset

Chapter 3: Hip Hop
41) Rhythm Index (quarter note equals 87)
42) Click, Doumbek (Intro)
43) Click, Metal Guiro (Intro, A Sections)
44) Click, Factory Metal (Intro)
45) Click, Drumset (A Sections)
46) Click, Tubano (B Sections)
47) Click, Afuche-Cabasa (B Sections)
48) Click, Drumset (B Sections)
49) Click, Drumset (Break in 7/8)
50) Click Subdivision Demonstration in 7/8
51) Click, Drumset (End Break)
52) Chart with Drumset
53) Chart without Drumset
54) Chart without Drumset and Loops

CHAPTER 1: BLUES/JAZZ

Blues

The most common blues form is the 12-bar blues. The blues song form can be played with different drumset grooves such as the shuffle, jazz-swing, 12/8 feel, funk, rock, mambo, cha cha, among others. The less common blues forms are the 8-bar blues (sometimes used in rock 'n' roll), 16-bar blues, or 18-bar blues (sometimes used in jazz with chord substitutions). The Blues is a melancholic music of Afro-American folk origin.

Blues artists to listen to are Muddy Waters, John Lee Hooker, Willie Dixon, B.B. King, T-Bone Walker, Albert Collins, Buddy Guy, and Eric Clapton, among others.

Jazz

Jazz is a musical art form that originated in New Orleans, Louisiana, in the United States around the start of the 20th century. Jazz is rooted in the blues and uses improvisation, swing, call-and-response, polyrhythms, syncopated phrases; it blends African-American music styles with western music theory and technique. Jazz is influenced by West African cultural and musical traditions brought to America by black musicians that evolved as they migrated from rural areas to larger cities. The jazz drumming style is rhythmically improvisational and is based on a quarter-note pulse with an underlying triplet feel.

Jazz artists to listen to are Charlie Parker, Dizzy Gillespie, Miles Davis, John Coltrane, Art Blakey, Max Roach, Philly Joe Jones, Elvin Jones, Tony Williams, Charles Mingus, Thelonious Monk, Chick Corea, and Herbie Hancock, among others.

Rhythm Index

The Rhythm Index is a breakdown of rhythms from the Blues/Jazz percussion score written in common time (4/4). *Common time* means there are four beats per measure, and the quarter note gets the beat (pulse).

Listen to each two-bar example, then answer the rhythm played in the next two bars while tapping your foot to the quarter note pulse. The fourteen examples will take you through the entire Rhythm Index and will help build your rhythmic vocabulary. Playing (locking in) with the click will help you to develop a strong time-feel.

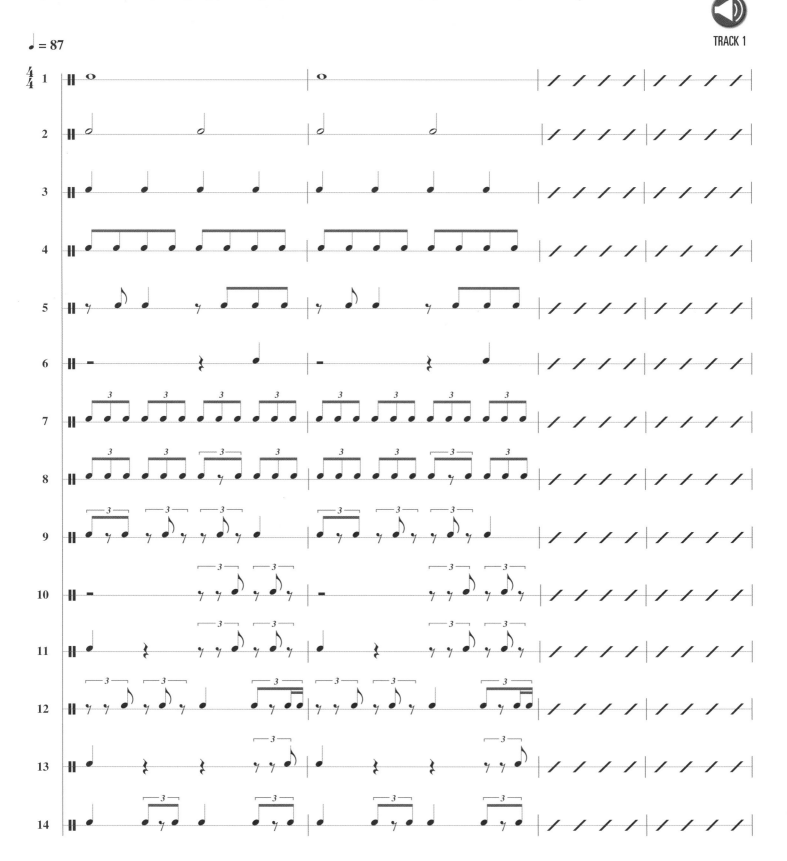

TRACK 1

Now that you're familiar with the rhythms included in the percussion score, play one rhythm into the next, and then play the bars at random one after another while tapping quarter notes with your foot. This will help you to develop improvising skills to be used with the score. Use the worksheet on the following page to document your own rhythms. Experiment with different tempos and dynamics.

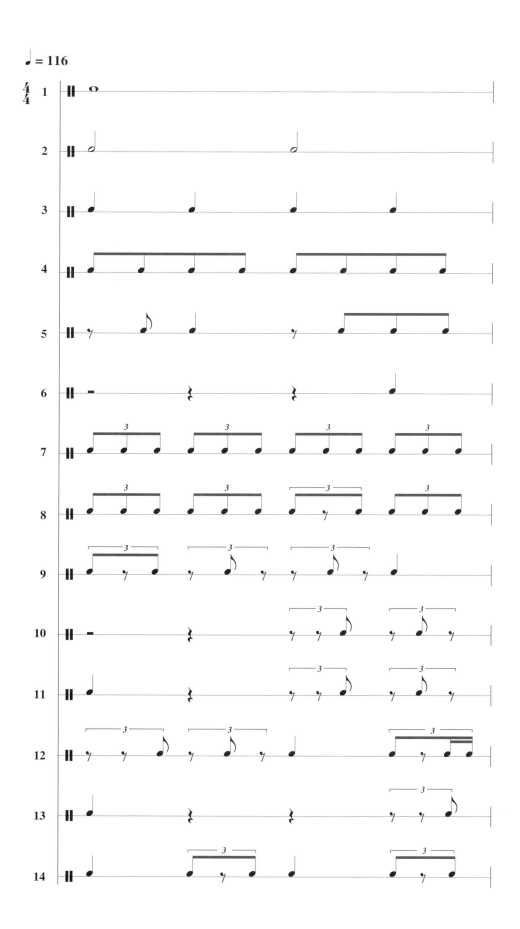

Worksheet

Blues/Jazz Score and Percussion Break Section

The Blues/Jazz score shows all the percussion and drumset parts that are featured demonstrations on tracks 2–20 and played on the chart (tracks 19 and 20). Note that the Percussion Break section of the score changes to a 6/8 time signature with a Latin feel. The D section is a common time feel (4/4) that is sub-divided into 3/4–3/4–2/4 over two measures of 4/4 time. The E section has a double time swing feel.

Take the time to learn the following demonstrations and concentrate on your time-feel, different tempos, and dynamics. After mastering the parts in the percussion score, return to the worksheet and write your own rhythms that can be applied to the score.

Intro and A Section

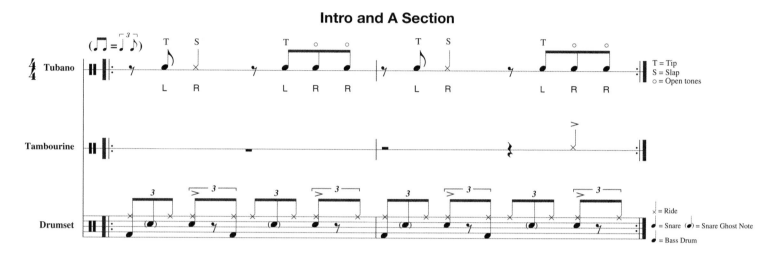

B Section

D Section

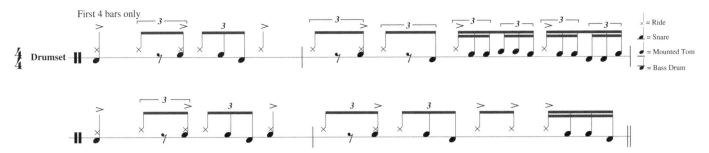

E Section

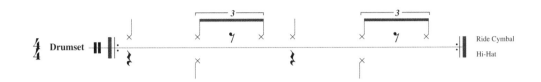

Percussion Break

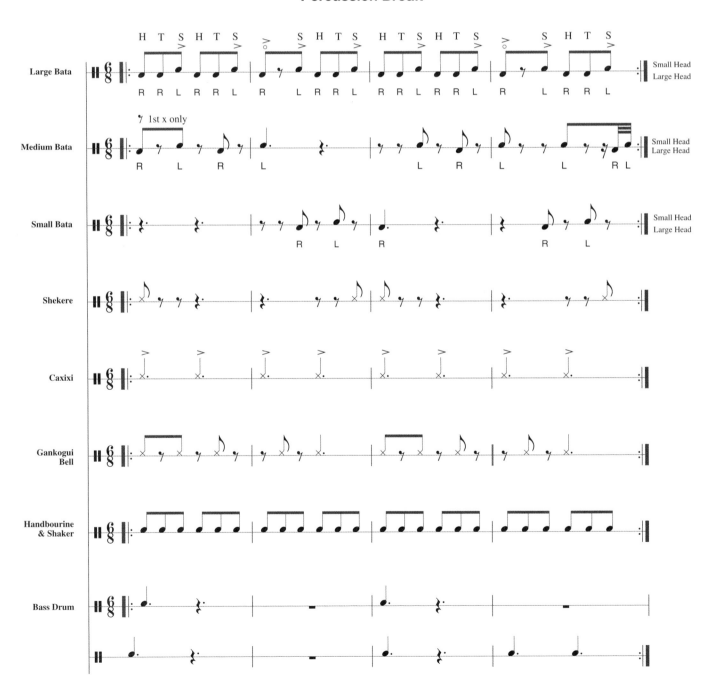

Instrument Demonstrations

The following demonstrations are examples of the basic technique and rhythms used for each percussion instrument played in the Blues/Jazz score. Refer to CD tracks 2–17.

Drumset

Percussion instruments have existed worldwide since 6000 B.C. The drumset was invented in the nineteenth century. Once the bass drum pedal was invented, a single person could play multiple percussion parts simultaneously. The drumset took off with a bang at the beginning of the twentieth century, when it was added to the jazz ensemble.

The standard drumset consists of a bass drum, snare drum, two tom toms, hi-hat cymbals, ride cymbal, and two crash cymbals. Sizes vary considerably from 24"–18" bass drums, 8"–18" toms, and 10"–14" snare drums. Drummers such as Louie Bellson, Keith Moon, Ginger Baker, and Billy Cobham pioneered double bass drum techniques. Rock drummers at times used large tom and cymbal setups. As calfskin drumheads were replaced with plastic heads, a large variety of drum sticks and brushes were invented. Cymbals and gongs were made of different types of metals or alloys such as brass, copper, bronze, tin, nickel, and zinc.

Some drummers use triggers in their drumset and external pads to trigger samplers, loops, and other midi devices.

Listen to the drumset demonstrations on tracks 2 (Intro, A section), 5 (B section), 16 (D section), and 17 (E section). Then play along with the Blues/Jazz Chart on track 20.

Tambourine

The tambourine is a hand-held (or stand-mounted) percussion instrument consisting of a wood or plastic frame with pairs of brass or nickel-plated steel alloy jingles. It can be played in several different ways, from shaking it to using an "arm and wrist motion." The hip, leg, hand, or stick can be used to strike it, resulting in accented notes. Many different shapes, types, and sizes of tambourines are manufactured that can be heard in popular, folk, and ethnic styles of music. The traditional tunable and non-tunable tambourine drumheads are made of calf-skin, goat-skin, or plastic.

Listen to the tambourine demonstrations on tracks 3 (Intro and A sections) and 6 (B sections) and then play along with track 19.

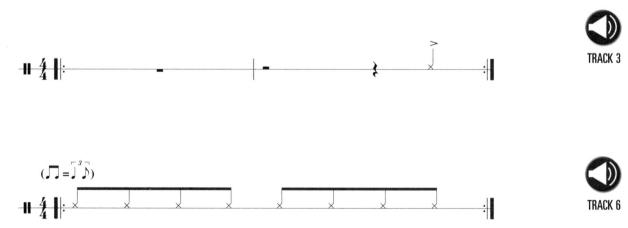

TRACK 3

TRACK 6

Tubano

The tubano, created by Remo, has a conga-like sound. They come in three different sizes (10", 12", and 14") and feature (key-tuned) NuSkyn heads that have a calf-like feel and sound. The traditional Cuban conga was made out of olive barrels or steamed bent staves of wood glued together. The heads were made of calf or buffalo skin and tacked to the wood. The tubano's innovative design features an internal resonating tube and cut-out feet to allow full bass resonance without using a floor stand or tilting the drum.

There is a broad range of sounds that can be produced depending on the hand position and where the drumhead is struck. One sound is the bass tone, the lowest frequency of the drum, which can be produced by hitting the center of the drumhead with the palm or fist. The open tones (see figure 1) can be achieved by playing with the fingers and palm towards the edge of the drumhead. The slap is a sharp defined sound, which can be played muted (see figure 2) or open.

Listen to the 12" tubano demonstration on track 4 (Intro and A sections) and then play along with track 19 or 20.

TRACK 4

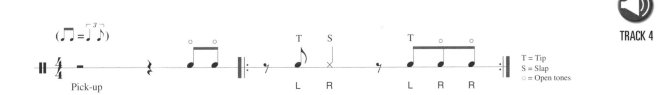

T = Tip
S = Slap
○ = Open tones

Conga and Tumbadora

Figure 1

Figure 2

Figure 3

Figure 4

Figure 5

The conga, coming from African and Cuban influences, has played a major role in modern music. These drums of African origin, first used by religious groups, are now very common in Afro-Cuban, Latin, and pop music.

The traditional Cuban conga was made out of olive barrels or steamed bent staves of wood glued together. The heads were made of calf or buffalo skin and tacked to the wood.

The smallest of the congas is called the "quinto" (30" x 11"); the middle one is called "conga," "seguidor," or "tres golpes" (30" x 11 ¾"); and the largest is called "tumbadora" or "salidor" (30" x 13"). Remo makes a "super tumba" (30" x 13") as well as the common sizes.

Among the most popular of the hand drums, the conga has a rich history due to its flexible tonal range and playability, and is widely used in drum circles.

There is a broad range of sounds that can be produced depending on the hand position and where the drumhead is struck. To produce the lowest sounding frequency, strike the center of the drumhead with the hand or palm (see figure 1). The middle tenor or open tone (see figure 2) can be achieved by playing with the fingers and palm towards the edge of the drum. The slap is a sharp defined sound, which can be played muted (see figure 3), open, or closed. The heel-toe technique—rocking between the palm (see figure 4) and the fingers (see figure 5)—consists of all muted strokes.

Listen to the conga and tumbadora demonstrations in the (B sections) on track 7 and then play along with track 19.

TRACK 7

T = Tip
S = Slap
H = Heel
○ = Open tones

Bass Drum

The bass drum is the largest and deepest sounding drum in the orchestra, and the heartbeat of the drumset. The drumset player strikes the kick drum by depressing a foot pedal attached to a bass drum beater. Bass drums are tuned with a proposed style of music in mind. For example, to get a rock sound, the tuning should be low, flat, and punchy, whereas a higher, more open-pitched tuning may be appropriate for playing jazz. The size of a bass drum can range from 16" to 24" in diameter with a depth of 14" to 18".

Two other types of bass drums are the pitched bass and the concert bass. The pitched bass drum is most commonly used in marching bands and drum corps where it is played with one or two large mallets. These drums are usually seen in a section of three to six bass drums. The concert bass drum is a pitched bass drum that is played with a large, fluffy mallet. This drum is usually heard in orchestral music or concert bands and is the largest drum in the orchestra.

Listen to the bass drum 2 demonstration on track 8 (Percussion Break) and then play along with track 19.

TRACK 8

Gankogui Bell

The gankogui (gon-KOE-gui) originated in Ghana and is a hand-forged iron bell. This bell is played with a wooden stick used to keep time in African drumming ensembles. The photograph is a gankogui bell manufactured by Remo. Similar to the Brazilian ago-ago bells, one gankogui actually consists of two bells. The smaller, higher-pitched bell is tuned approximately one octave, or a third, below the larger bell.

Listen to the gankogui bell demonstration for the Percussion Break on track 9 and then play along with track 19.

TRACK 9

Shekere

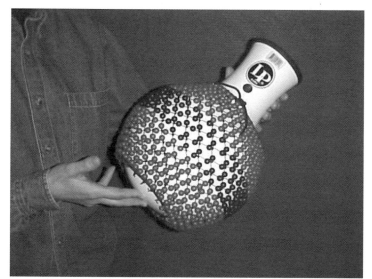

Figure 1

Figure 2

The shekere is a natural, hollowed gourd covered with an intricate net of pearls, seeds, stones, or beads. Each gourd is individually unique and varies slightly in sound and size. The gourds are opened, cleaned, and scraped, and then the inside of the gourd is sealed with polyurethane, which increases the resonance and tone of the instrument. The outside of the gourd is finished with a stain or painted and wrapped with a net of beadwork. Other materials used to make shekeres are plastic, metal, or fiberglass. The shekere in the photograph is a fiberglass body wrapped in plastic beads called the LP Pro created by Latin Percussion.

The shekere is widely used in many African cultures as a dance rhythm instrument. The instrument is played by a combination of up (see figure 1) and down (see figure 2) shaking and bouncing between the hands. Striking the bottom of the shekere with the palm will produce bass tones.

Listen to the shekere demonstration for the Percussion Break on track 10 and then play along with track 19.

TRACK 10

Bata Drums

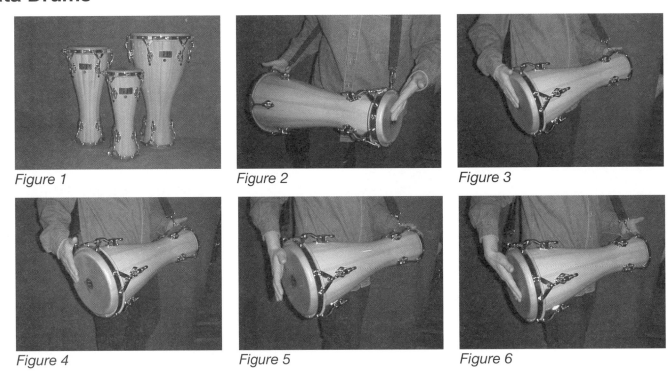

Figure 1

Figure 2

Figure 3

Figure 4

Figure 5

Figure 6

The bata drums are a set of sacred, two-headed drums played in Cuba. The ensemble is made up of three drums (see figure 1): Okonkolo is the smallest, the middle drum is the Itotele, and the large drum is Iya. Traditionally, the batas are ceremonial drums played in a "call-and-response" rhythmic style. The origins of the ceremonies are found within the traditional religion of the Yoruba people of West Africa.

The small drum plays more of an ostinato figure as a timekeeper, while the middle drum improvises. The large drum leads by signaling the section changes and the call for conversation with the middle drum.

The low-pitched head is played by the right hand, and the high-pitched head is played with the left hand. The small head of the drum is struck with a quick, twisting motion of the wrist and forearm, which produces the slap sound (see figure 2). There are two techniques used in playing the large head that result in either an open or muted tone. The muted, or closed tones (see figure 3), are played by striking the drum and leaving the hand on the head. To play open tones, strike the head and lift the hand off of the drumhead (see figure 4). The tap stroke is a time keeping technique similar to the heel-toe motion used when playing conga drums (see figures 5 and 6).

Listen to the large bata demonstration in the Percussion Break on track 11, medium bata demonstration in the Percussion Break on track 12, and the small bata demonstration in the Percussion Break on track 13, and then play along with track 19.

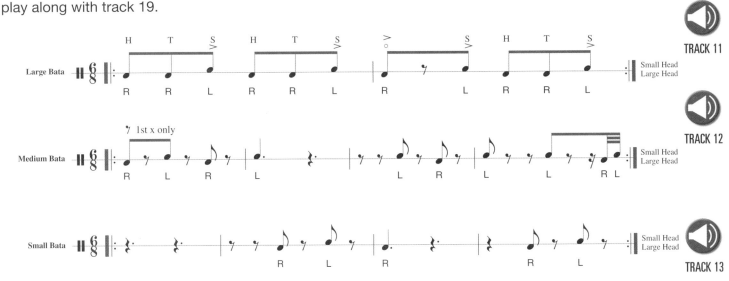

TRACK 11

TRACK 12

TRACK 13

Handbourine and Shaker

Handbourine

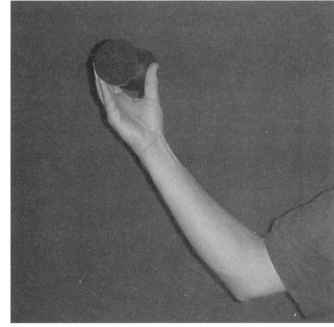

Shaker

The handbourine stick (manufactured by Regal Tip) is derived from the traditional tambourine. The stick has tambourine jingles that loosely move back and fourth. The shaker (manufactured by LP) is made of plastic or metal and is filled with very small beads that produce a sharp and distinct sound. Both instruments played in unison create a unique sound.

Listen to the handbourine and shaker demonstration played in unison on track 14 (Percussion Break) and play along with track 19. The phrase has no accents, therefore requires less motion.

TRACK 14

Caxixi (Baskets)

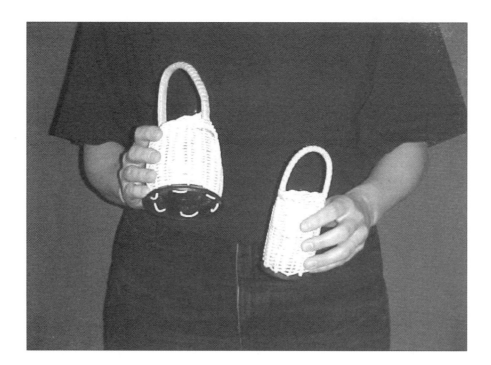

Caxixi are woven baskets of grass or cane containing small rattles. The bottom surface of the basket is made of gourd, metal, or plastic. The material inside striking the bottom surface of the basket produces the tone. The baskets (one small and one large) are held in each hand and traditionally played with a vertical motion (see photo) as opposed to the horizontal motion of a shaker, providing a different, softer sound.

Listen to the caxixi demonstration on track 15 (Percussion Break, Section C2) and then play along with track 19.

TRACK 15

Blues/Jazz Break

Listen to the unison break on track 19 and then play along with track 20. The quarter note becomes the dotted quarter note in the 6/8 time signature, but the eighth note stays the same. There are six beats per measure, and the eighth note gets the beat (pulse). Practice this phrase while tapping the dotted quarter-note pulse with your foot.

It is important to memorize the phrasing of the break before you play with the chart. Check out the unison ending on track 18.

TRACK 18

Blues/Jazz Chart

Now that you've learned the Blues/Jazz score and percussion break section, listen to the entire composition on track 19 (with drumset) and play along with the percussion instrument you've been working on. Then, learn a different instrument and play along with the ensemble.

When you are ready to play drumset with the composition, play along with track 20.

TRACK 19
w/ drumset

TRACK 20
w/out drumset

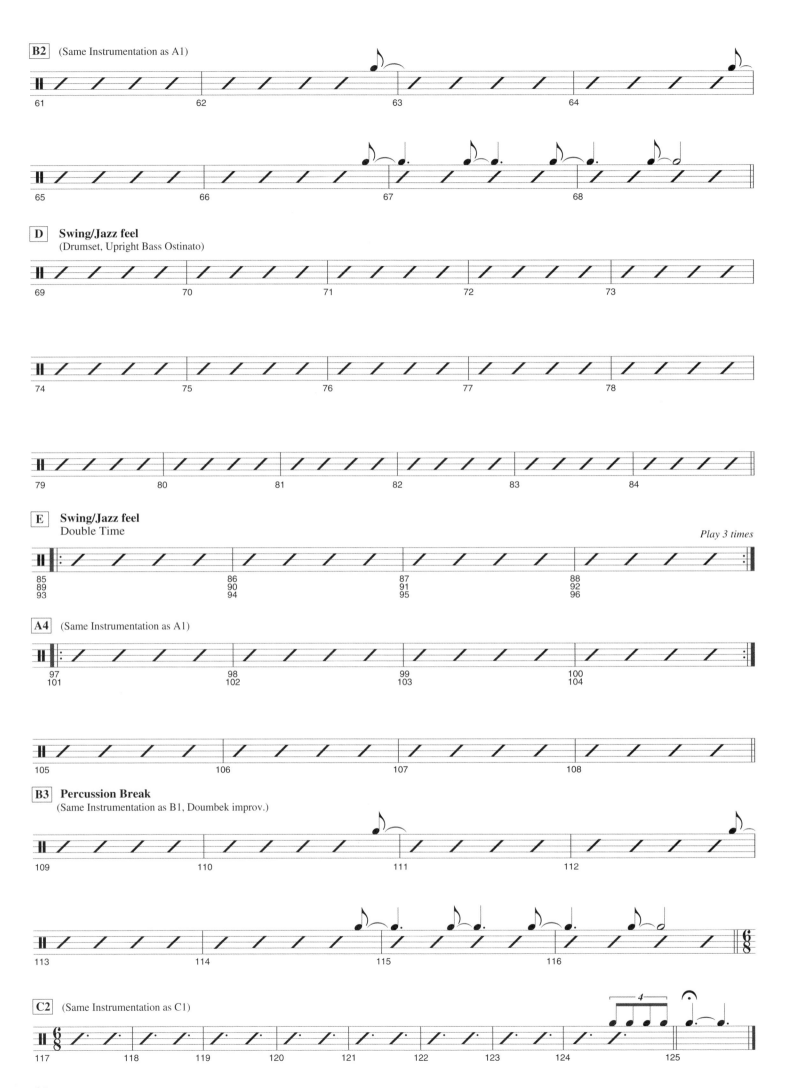

CHAPTER 2:
BO DIDDLEY/SECOND LINE/ROCK

Bo Diddley

The "Bo Diddley" is a two-bar phrase, rhumba-like beat outlined by the Cuban 3-2 son clave. The unique sound of the Bo Diddley groove is mainly played between the high tom, floor tom, and snare drum, while the bass drum outlines the clave rhythm. The groove is based on the sixteenth note, but the quarter-note pulse anchors the syncopated rhythm. Bo Diddley created this style using a hard-edged guitar sound. His influence as an American singer/songwriter and guitarist is often cited as a key element in the transition of blues into rock 'n' roll.

Second Line

The New Orleans second line style of drumming is heavily influenced by military marches, carnival street beats, and a tradition in brass band parades. As part of the traditional New Orleans culture, the second line is often played during funeral processions. Once the church service is over, the band plays sad hymns and dirges as they make their way to the cemetery sight. On the way back, the second line is incorporated as the music becomes joyful and people dance, sport umbrellas, and wave their handkerchiefs. The second line is a way for mourners to send off their departed family members and friends in "style," sometimes referred to as a "jazz funeral."

Rock

In the early to mid-1950s, the musical style of rock 'n' roll was born in the United States. Rock 'n' roll is an Afro-American style of music that evolved from a handful of popular genres starting with folk music, blues, boogie woogie, gospel, jump blues, and rhythm 'n' blues. Along with the African-American influence, it also drew on country and western music while mixing in European melodies.

Rock drumming is based on a consistent eighth-note pulse with the snare drum typically playing a strong back beat on two and four. The bass drum rhythm varies depending on the figure played by the bass guitar.

Rock 'n' roll artists such as Chuck Berry, Little Richard, Bo Diddley, The Platters, Fats Domino, and Carl Perkins usually played to African-American crowds. While these trailblazing early rockers were indisposed to racism, local authorities and dance halls were very much divided upon racial lines.

Mainstream acceptance of rock 'n' roll came during the mid-1950s through radio play, phonographs, and juke-boxes in dance halls and clubs. Artist such as Elvis Presley, Bill Haley and the Comets, Buddy Holly, The Big Bopper, Jerry Lee Lewis, and Johnny Cash often toured together and mainly played to young audiences across the U.S. and Great Britain.

Throughout the 1960s, groups such as The Animals, The Rolling Stones, and The Beatles increasingly showed blues influences, characterized by the use of electric guitar riffs and relatively simple phrase structure.

The Yardbirds and The Kinks, followed by The Who with drummer Keith Moon, represented the new Mod style. Towards the end of the decade, British and American rock groups began to explore psychedelic musical styles that made reference to the hallucinogenic experiences of a prominent drug sub-culture.

Rhythm Index

The Rhythm Index is a breakdown of rhythms from the Bo Diddley percussion score written in common time (4/4). *Common time* means there are four beats per measure, and the quarter note gets the beat (pulse).

Listen to each two-bar example on track 21, then answer the rhythm played during the next two bars while tapping your foot to the quarter-note pulse. The twenty-seven examples will take you through the entire Rhythm Index and will help build your rhythmic vocabulary. Playing (locking in) with the click will help you to develop a strong time-feel.

TRACK 21

Now that you're familiar with the rhythms included in the percussion score, play one rhythm into the next, and then play the bars at random one after another while tapping the quarter notes with your foot. This will help you to develop improvising skills to be used with the score. Use the worksheet on the following page to document your own rhythms. Experiment with different tempos and dynamics.

Worksheet

Bo Diddley Score and Percussion Break Section

The Bo Diddley score shows all the percussion and drumset parts that are featured demonstrations on tracks 21–40 and played on the Bo Diddley charts on tracks 39 and 40.

Take the time to learn the following demonstrations and concentrate on your time-feel, different tempos, and dynamics. After mastering the parts in the percussion score, return to the worksheet and write your own rhythms that can be applied to the score.

Intro & Intrerlude Sections

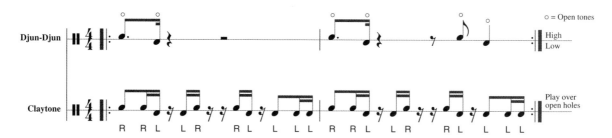

A Sections

Break

B Sections

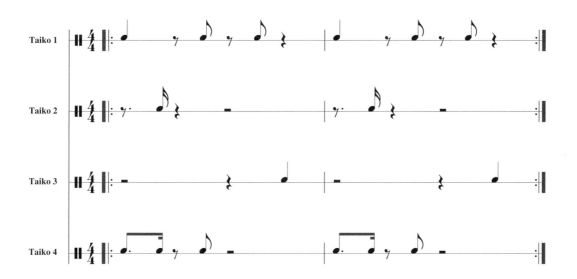

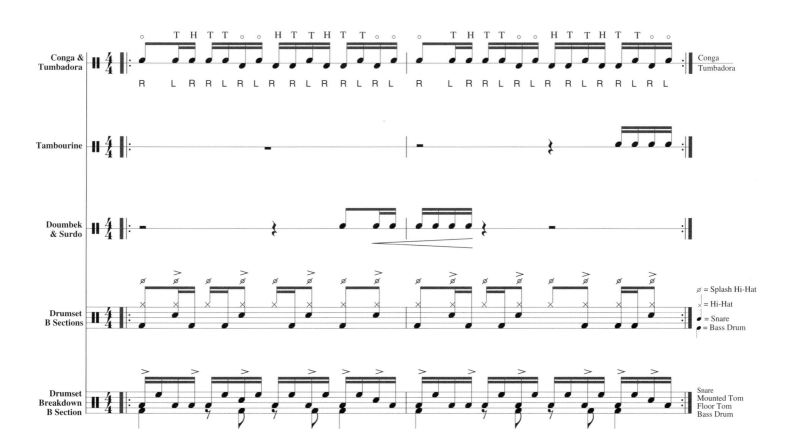

Clay/Udu Drums

Figure 1

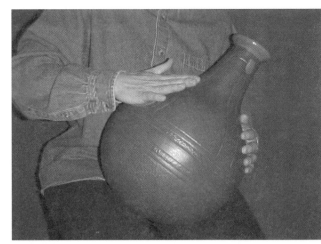

Figure 2

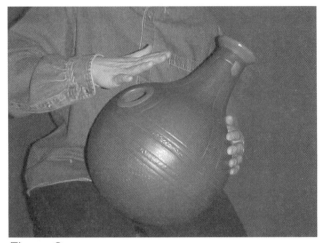

Figure 3

Figure 4

Clay and Udu drums (see figure 1) are made of clay with a round hole on the body of the drum and an opening at the top of a narrow vase-like vessel. The playing techniques vary depending on the player and particular region, and neither drum has a head or membrane as a playing surface. These drums derived from the traditional Nigerian water pot and were played by women for ceremonial music. When used in religious ceremonies, some believe the deep haunting sounds are voices of their ancestors.

The basic technique incorporates drumming on the side and top hole (with the palm of both hands), while opening and closing the holes to move air through the chamber (see figure 2). Varying the strokes and release of the hands will allow the player to create different tonal variations from the instrument (see figure 3). The sound is a combination of bent and round harmonious bass tones that have tabla-like qualities. The body or shell of the drum can also be played with fingers to create slap tones and clay percussive sound types (see figure 4). The photographs feature claytone drums manufactured by Latin Percussion developed in partnership with Frank Giorgini.

Listen to the claytone (Intro and Interlude sections) demonstration on track 22 and then play along with track 39.

TRACK 22

Djun-Djun

The djun-djun is a large two-headed African drum made from a wooden or metal shell (such as hollowed logs or oil cans). They serve as the beat-keepers in drum circles and are native to the region of West Africa. The drums are low-pitched and very similar to the bass drum, providing the rhythmic and melodic base to the djembe orchestra. In some regions the drums are played horizontally with a stick in one hand while the other hand strikes a bell with a metal stick. The djun-djun often plays an *ostinato* part (repetitive part).

In the following example, a 14" and 16" djun-djun is being played with two mallets as shown in the photograph. The drums vary in sizes from 12 inches to 22 inches.

Listen to the djun-djun demonstration on track 23 (Intro and Interlude sections) and play along with track 39.

TRACK 23

○ = Open tones

High

Low

Tambourine

The tambourine is a hand-held (or stand-mounted) percussion instrument consisting of a wood or plastic frame with pairs of brass or nickel-plated steel alloy jingles. It can be played in several different ways, from shaking it to using an "arm and wrist motion." The hip, leg, hand, or stick can be used to strike it, resulting in accented notes. Many different shapes, types, and sizes of tambourines are manufactured and can be heard in popular, folk, and ethnic styles of music. The traditional tunable and non-tunable tambourine drumheads consist of calf-skin, goat-skin, or plastic.

Listen to the tambourine demonstrations on tracks 24 (A sections) and 33 (B sections), and then play along with track 39.

TRACK 24

TRACK 33

Rainstick (Shaker)

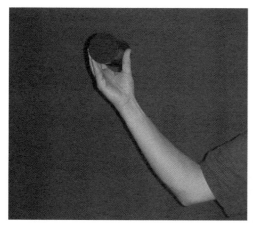

Figure 1

Figure 2

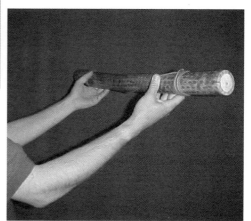

Figure 3

The rainstick is traditionally made from the skeleton of a dead cactus plant. The interior structure of the hollow cylinder contains various types of thorns, bamboo, cactus spines, or wooden pegs which divert the pebbles, rice, or seeds as they roll and trickle in a spiral formation to create the sound of gentle rain. Legend has it that the rainstick was used as a ceremonial instrument to invoke rainy weather. The rainstick can also be used as a shaker (see figures 2 and 3). Both the rainstick and the shaker can be used for sound effects by shaking the instrument with a swift motion. Different techniques can be used to play the shaker (see figure 1) using one or two hands, while the rainstick (see figure 2 and 3) is held with both hands together.

The motion used will affect the overall feel and can be played with or without accents. Accented notes require a broader movement, and unaccented notes utilize less motion.

Listen to the rainstick demonstration on track 25 (A sections) and then play along with track 39.

TRACK 25

Drum Set

Percussion instruments have existed worldwide since 6000 B.C. The drumset was invented in the nineteenth century. Once the bass drum pedal was invented, a single person could play multiple percussion parts simultaneously. The drumset took off with a bang at the beginning of the twentieth century, when it was added to the jazz ensemble.

The standard drumset consists of a bass drum, snare drum, two tom toms, hi-hat cymbals, ride cymbal, and two crash cymbals. Sizes vary considerably from 24"–18" bass drums, 8"–18" toms, and 10"–14" snare drums. Drummers such as Louie Bellson, Keith Moon, Ginger Baker, and Billy Cobham pioneered double bass drum techniques. Rock drummers at times used large tom and cymbal setups. As calfskin drumheads were replaced with plastic heads, a large variety of drum sticks and brushes were invented. Cymbals and gongs were made of different types of metals or alloys such as brass, copper, bronze, tin, nickel, and zinc.

Some drummers use triggers in their drumset and external pads to trigger samplers, loops, and other midi devices.

Listen to the drumset demonstration on tracks 26 (A section), 32 (B section), and 37 (B section, Bo Diddley Breakdown). Then play along with track 40.

36

Snare Drum

The snare drum is descended from military drums and is still associated with marching bands. The drum is played in a horizontal position, supported by a stand or hung at the player's side in a marching formation. Only the upper head is struck with wooden sticks. The bottom head has catgut or metal wires (*snares*) stretched across, which produce a rattling sound (when the drum is struck) as they vibrate against the head. Commonly, a lever on the side of the drum will loosen the snares, eliminating the rattle. Special effects played by the snare drum include playing with the snares off, using different types of sticks, playing the edge or middle of the head, and playing the rim. The shells as well as the hoops are commonly made of metal or wood.

Listen to the snare drum demonstration on track 27 (Break 1) and then play along with track 39.

TRACK 27

Doumbek

Figure 1

Figure 2

Figure 3

The doumbek (see figure 1) is a Middle Eastern hand drum, originally played in

Figure 4

Egypt, Turkey, and Armenia. In many Middle Eastern cultures they serve as the main drums for classical and theatrical music, as well as popular music. The doumbek's clear sound and combination of deep and high tone have made it a popular drum for belly dancing and drum circles. It's also used in the Sufi tradition to put people in a trance.

The doumbek has three basic sounds: *dum* is the bass tone played with your left hand in the middle of the drum (see figure 1). *Tek* is a high ringing sound played with your right hand (see figure 2). The tone is produced by striking the outside edge of the head where the edge of the drum and the skin meet. *Ka* is the same sound as tek, but played with your left hand (see figure 3). Figure 4 shows a hybrid slap position.

Traditionally the doumbek is played while seated. The drum is placed in your lap with the head of the drum facing your right leg. Rest your left hand on top of the drum for support. If this seems uncomfortable, try placing the drum between your legs while sitting (see figure 1) or standing. Another method is to weave a shoulder strap through the lacing; this is a great way to carry the drum and play at the same time. The doumbek is a hand drum and should never be played with a stick or mallet of any kind. It's also important to remember to remove your rings before playing. Some additional notes on tuning can be found on page 55.

Listen to the doumbek demonstrations on tracks 28 (Break 1) and 35 (B sections), and then play along with track 39.

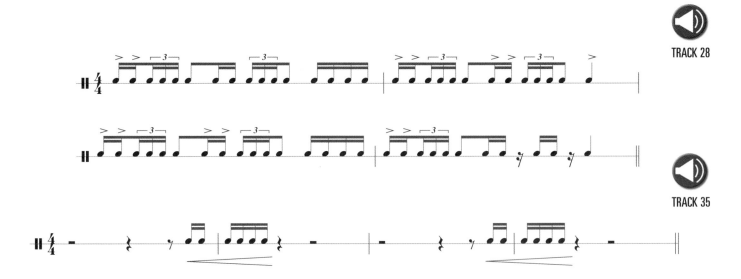

TRACK 28

TRACK 35

Bongos

The bongos emerged from the Afro-Cuban and Spanish musical styles of Cuba called changui and son. Consisting of two high-pitched drums of different sizes joined by a wooden bridge, they are often tuned a fifth apart. Bongo drums are made of wood or fiberglass and the heads are usually made of animal skin or synthetic materials.

Traditionally, the bongos are played in a seated position while tightly holding them between the knees or set on a stand. The large 8" drum played on the right side is referred to as *macho* (Spanish for male) and the small 6" drum played on the left side is called *hembra* (Spanish for female). Although the drums are usually played with the fingers and hands, mallets and other sticks can be used to produce specific sound effects.

Listen to the bongo demonstration on track 28 (Break 1) and then play along with track 39.

TRACK 28

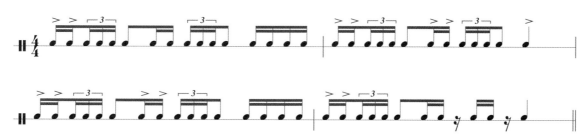

Metal Guiro

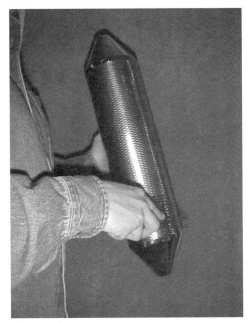
Figure 1

Figure 2

The metal guiro is a cylinder-shaped instrument played with a metal pick. The traditional gourd guiros are commonly played in many Latin-American musical styles and come in a variety of sizes. Metal guiros are most commonly used to play the merengue style of the Dominican Republic. It produces a brighter and louder sound than the wood of traditional Cuban gourd guiros. Metal guiros are made of a lightweight metal with a stainless steel surface. The surface can vary from fine to coarse texture or large raised grooves. There are a variety of scrapers including a single metal wire, a multi-wire, prong metal, a short metal stick, or a metal pick.

The technique used to play the guiro is involved, but in basic terms, the motion can be described as a sweeping and scraping of up and downstrokes (see figures 1 and 2).

TRACK 29

Listen for the metal guiro demonstration on track 29 (Break 1). It's behind the ago-sha, so listen carefully. Once you have the part in your head, play along with track 39.

Ago-Sha

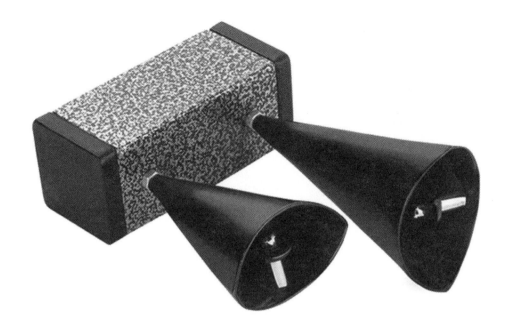

The ago-sha is a hybrid instrument that combines an ago-go bell with a ganza or shaker. This all-in-one instrument has a built-in striker on the inside of the ago-sha bell that strikes the bell as you move the instrument back and forth to produce its unique sound.

Listen to the ago-sha demonstration on track 29 (Break 1) and then play along with track 39.

TRACK 29

Pick-up

Suspended Cymbal

The twenty-inch light ride can be described as silvery and full, with a chimer capable of a wide range of sounds. It has a very responsive, soft feel and has a slightly papery, yet sparkling stick sound over a foggy wash. It is a dynamic ride for any application, but especially for lower volume situations. It is commonly used in blues, jazz, country, and acoustic or vocal-oriented music.

The scrape technique can be played with any metal rod (i.e. triangle rod or the metal part of brushes). Listen to the suspended cymbal demonstration on track 31 (Break 1) and then play along with track 39.

TRACK 31

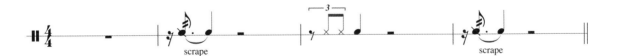

Remo Gong Drum

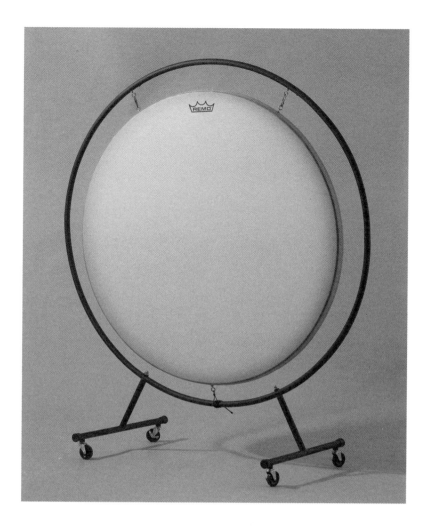

The Remo gong drums are a series of unique tunable percussion instruments for use in a wide range of playing situations. The tunable gong drum is constructed using Remo's proprietary aluminum, ABS large frame ring, and RENAISSANCE® drumhead film.

The sizes of the Gong Drums are 32", 46", or 60" in diameter. The look and sound of these instruments are quite unique. This tunable drum is suspended from a steel frame on wheels, making it easy to move. The fundamental tone is very low and is achieved by striking the center of the drum. In contrast, a very high sound will resonate from striking the edge of the drum.

Listen to the gong demonstration on track 30 (Break 1) and then play along with track 39.

TRACK 30

Conga and Tumbadora

Figure 1

Figure 2

Figure 3

Figure 4

Figure 5

The conga, coming from African and Cuban influences, has played a major role in modern music. These drums of African origin, first used by religious groups, are now very common in Afro-Cuban, Latin, and pop music.

The traditional Cuban conga was made out of olive barrels or steamed bent staves of wood glued together. The heads were made of calf or buffalo skin and tacked to the wood.

The smallest of the congas is called the "quinto" (30" x 11"); the middle one is called "conga," "seguidor," or "tres golpes" (30" x 11 ¾"); and the largest is called "tumbadora" or "salidor" (30" x 13"). Remo makes a "super tumba" (30" x 13"), as well as the common sizes.

Among the most popular of the hand drums, the conga drum has a rich history due to its flexible tonal range and playability, and it is widely used in drum circles.

There is a broad range of sounds that can be produced depending on the hand position and where the drum-head is struck. To produce the lowest sounding frequency, strike the center of the drumhead with the hand or palm (see figure 1). The middle tenor or open tone (see figure 2) can be achieved by playing with the fingers and palm towards the edge of the drum. The slap is a sharp defined sound, which can be played muted (see figure 3), open, or closed. The heel-toe technique—rocking between the palm (see figure 4) and the fingers (see figure 5)—consists of all muted strokes.

Listen to the conga and tumbadora demonstration in the (B sections) on track 34 and then play along with track 39.

TRACK 34

Surdo

Figure 1

Figure 2

The surdo is the pulse and provides the bottom or bass tone for the percussion ensemble. Surdos are large two-headed (top and bottom) drums usually made of wood or metal and are played with a soft mallet. While the mallet in one hand plays the accented notes (see figure1), the other hand plays muted or *ghost notes* (see figure 2) to accompany the main pulse.

The surdo comes in a variety of sizes, categorized as small, medium, and large. The surdo marcana is the largest of the three drums, and the approximate sizes are 24" x 20", 22" x 24", and 20" x 22" (an 18-inch or 16-inch floor tom can be used as a substitute for the large surdo). The contra surdo is the medium drum and the sizes are approximately 15 x 16, 16 x 18, and 18 x 16 (a 14" or 13" tom tom can be used as a substitute for the medium surdo). The surdo cortador is the smallest of the three, and the sizes vary from 12 x 13 to 13 x 14 (a 12" or 10" tom tom can be used as a substitute for the small surdo).

Listen to the surdo demonstrations on tracks 27 (Break 1) and 36 (B sections), and then play along with track 39.

TRACK 27

TRACK 36

Taiko Drums

Taiko drums and taiko drumming derive from the Japanese art form of folk and classical musical traditions. The drums are double-headed, barrel-shaped, and are played with different types of wooden sticks specific to each drum. The drums come in several sizes ranging from small to very large and are high-tension tuned. Taiko performances can be heard in shrines and temples, traditional festivals, and in concerts of ensemble music.

Remo's Taiko drums are inspired by a long-honored Japanese drumming heritage. They carefully follow authentic Japanese designs from the barrel-shaped Nagado Daiko to the contoured Shime Daiko. An Acousticon™ shell, durable TUFF-E-NUFF® finish, and Remo's Type 12 Nuskyn® Taiko heads have made these drums a powerful new choice for professionals, educators, and students. The large and small tunable Nagados are the first of their kind. They feature a heavy-duty tuning system, steel counterhoops, and replaceable drumheads. Pitch flexibility, combined with heads that can be changed in minutes instead of days, makes these drums both practical and inspiring.

Listen to the four taiko drums as they are demonstrated on track 38 (B sections) and then play along with track 39.

TRACK 38

Bo Diddley Chart

Now that you've learned the Bo Diddley score and percussion break section, listen to the entire composition on track 39 (with drumset) and then play along with the percussion instrument you've been working on. Then, learn a different instrument and play along with the ensemble.

When you are ready to play drumset with the composition, play along with track 40.

TRACK 39
w/ drumset

TRACK 40
w/out drumset

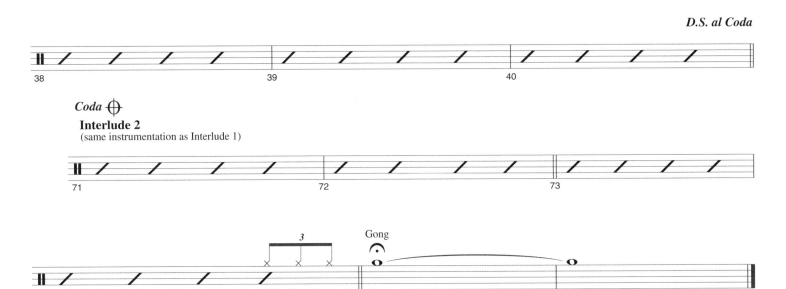

CHAPTER 3: HIP HOP

Hip Hop

The term "hip hop" comes from an urban lifestyle—a culture filled with graffiti, break dancing, and rapping all over a dance groove with a turntable scratching throughout. Hip hop is the culture from which rap emerged with its own language, style of dress, music, and state of mind that is constantly changing. Stylistically, the music often utilizes audio loops and programmed drum grooves created by sequencing software. Low-end bass sounds and synthesizers are commonly used to create a backdrop for a rap of rhythmic rhymes.

Rhythm Index

The Rhythm Index is a breakdown of rhythms from the hip hop percussion score written in common time (4/4). *Common* time means there are four beats per measure, and the quarter note gets the beat (pulse).

Listen to each two-bar example then answer the rhythm played in the next two bars while tapping your foot to the quarter-note pulse. The thirteen examples will take you through the entire Rhythm Index and will help build your rhythmic vocabulary. Playing (locking in) with the click will help you to develop a strong time-feel.

TRACK 41

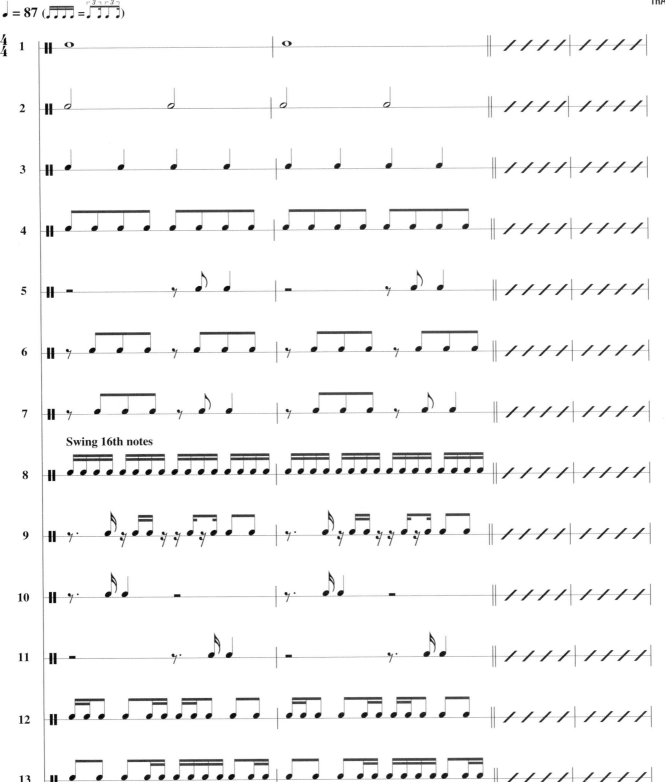

Now that you're familiar with the rhythms included in the percussion score, play one rhythm into the next, and then play the bars at random one after another while tapping the quarter-note pulse with your foot. This will help you to develop improvising skills to be used with the score. Use the worksheet on the following page to document your own rhythms. Experiment with different tempos and dynamics.

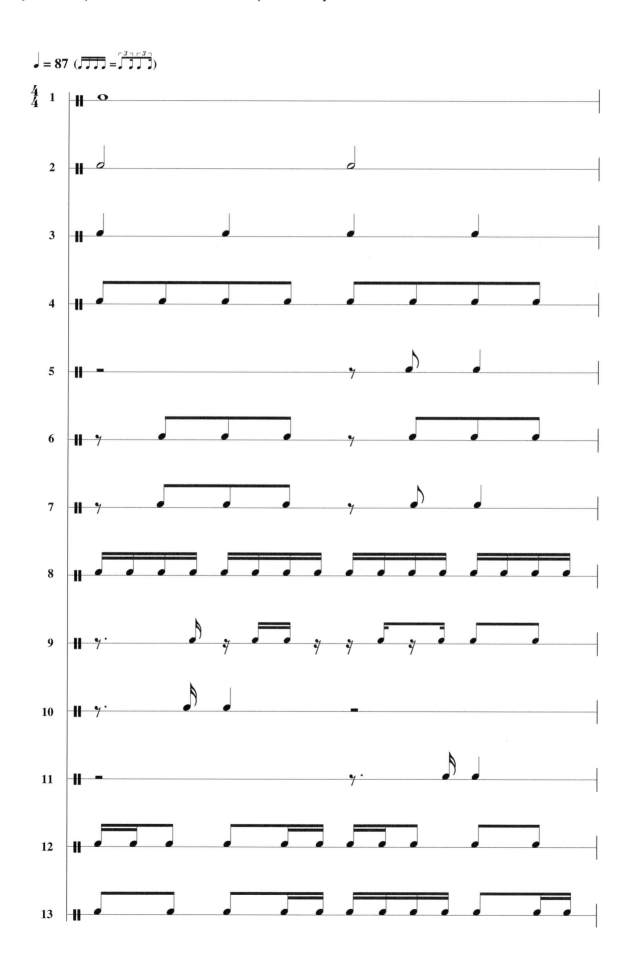

Worksheet

Hip Hop Score

The hip hop score shows all the percussion and drumset parts that are featured demonstrations on tracks 41-54 and played on the chart (tracks 52–54).

Take the time to learn the following demonstrations while concentrating on your time-feel, different tempos, and dynamics. After mastering the parts in the percussion score, return to the worksheet and write your own rhythms that can be applied to the score.

Intro and Interlude Sections

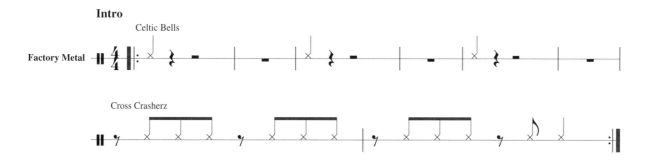

A Sections

B Sections

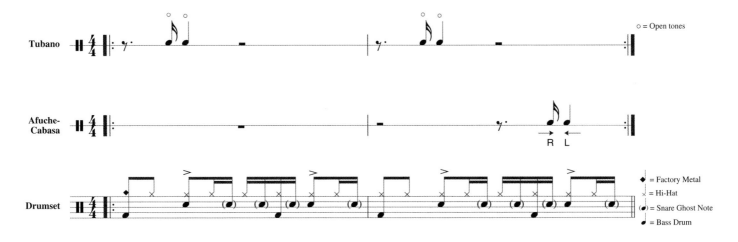

Drumset Break

Drumset End Break

Doumbek

Figure 1

Figure 2

Figure 3

The doumbek or darbukah (see figure 1) is a Middle Eastern hand drum, origi-nally played in Egypt, Turkey, and Armenia. In many Middle Eastern cultures they serve as the main drums for classical and theatrical music, as well as popular music. The doumbek's clear sound and combination of deep and high tone have made it a popular drum for belly dancing and drum circles. It's also used in the Sufi tradition to put people in a trance.

Figure 4

The doumbek has three basic sounds: *Dum* is the bass tone played with your left hand in the middle of the drum (see figure 1). *Tek* is a high ringing sound played with your right hand (see figure 2). The tone is produced by striking the outside edge of the head where the edge of the drum and the skin meet. Ka is the same sound as tek, but played with your left hand (see figure 3). Figure 4 shows a hybrid slap position.

Traditionally the doumbek is played while sitting down. The drum is placed in your lap with the head of the drum facing your right leg. Rest your left hand on top of the drum for support. If this seems uncomfortable, try placing the drum between your legs while sitting (see figure 1) or standing. A third method is to weave a shoulder strap through the lacing; this is a great way to carry the drum and play it at the same time. The doumbek is a hand drum and should never be played with a stick or mallet of any kind. It's also important to remember to remove your rings before playing.

A Note on Tuning

All goatskin drums are affected by humidity. When the weather is wet and humid, the skin soaks up the moisture, giving the drum a deeper bass sound. When the weather is dry the skin becomes dry, giving the drum a sharp ringing sound. If you feel that the goatskin on your doumbek has too much moisture in it, find a heat source such as the sun, a fire, or your stove. Even the warmth of your hand can help dry out a goatskin. It's important not to heat your drum too fast, though. Take your time and let the skin dry slowly.

Remo doumbeks are available in a tunable version with plastic heads, which allow the player pitch flexibility as well as the ability to change heads quickly. These doumbeks come in various sizes including 15" x 8", 16" x 9", 16" x 10", and 18" x 10".

Listen to the doumbek demonstrations on track 42 (Intro) and then play along with track 52.

TRACK 42

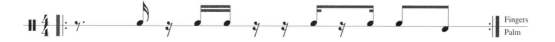

Metal Guiro

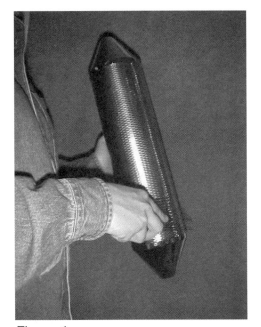

Figure 1

Figure 2

The metal guiro is a cylinder-shaped instrument played with a metal pick. The traditional gourd guiros are commonly played in many Latin-American musical styles and come in a variety of sizes. Metal guiros are most commonly used to play the merengue style of the Dominican Republic. It produces a brighter and louder sound than the wood of traditional Cuban gourd guiros. Metal guiros are made of a lightweight metal with a stainless steel surface. The surface can vary from fine to coarse texture or large raised grooves. There are a variety of scrapers including a single metal wire, a multi-wire, prong metal, a short metal stick, or a metal pick.

The technique used to play the guiro is involved, but in basic terms, the motion can be described as a sweeping and scraping of up and downstrokes (see figures 1 and 2).

Listen to the metal guiro demonstration on track 43 (Intro, Interlude, A sections and vocal trading section), and then play along with track 52.

TRACK 43

Scrape

Factory Metal (Celtic Bells and Cross Crasherz)

Figure 1

Figure 2

Factor metal percussion ProLine Celtic Bells (see figure 1) radiate a pure bell or cup chime tone with an edgy metallic bite. Available in 6-, 8-, 10-, and 12-inch sizes, the cross design creates an amazing spectrum of overtones, and each bell comes with interchangeable sizzlers and jingles which allow the user to customize effect sounds. Sizzlers and jingles can be used in multiple combinations to shape the bell sounds from bright and resonant to dry and trashy.

Sizzlers alone create a resonant rivet-type wash that extends the decay of the bell, brightening up the sustain and overall tone. Adding jingles will create a white noise effect—the more jingles used, the bigger the *bite* will be. The torque of the sizzlers and jingles can be adjusted from wet and bright, to short and trashy, depending on how they are individually tensioned.

Sets of stacked Celtic Bells create melodic playing combinations—easily stacked over the top of each other to conserve space. Whether played as singles or combined on MultiStackers, Celtic Bells offer a wide range of sound options for drummers and percussionists. The 6" and 8" sizes can be easily mounted to the hi-hat clutch, above the top cymbal, to double as a metallic hi-hat tambourine effect.

The Cross Crasherz (see figure 2) produces an amazing "white noise" attack with a unique metallic rattler effect. Fabricated from two alloy layers, this special effect is a result of four jingles sandwiched in between, giving it an extra layer of sonic depth. The Cross Crasherz decay and pitch can be adjusted by simply tightening one or all of the four tension screws that hold the cross plates together. Leaving the tension loose produces a shimmering metallic attack with long rattler sustain, while tighter tension adjustments produce sharper attacks and shorter sustain.

Listen to the Celtic Bells and Cross Crasherz demonstration on track 44 (Intro) and then play along with track 52.

TRACK 44

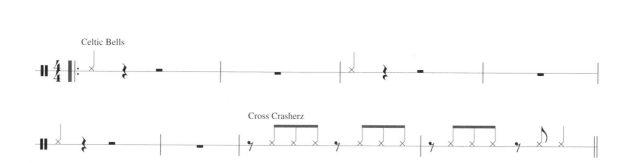

Drumset

Percussion instruments have existed worldwide since 6000 B.C. The drumset was invented in the nineteenth century. Once the bass drum pedal was invented, a single person to play multiple percussion parts simultaneously. The drumset took off with a bang at the beginning of the twentieth century, when it was added to the jazz ensemble.

The standard drumset consists of a bass drum, snare drum, two tom toms, hi-hat cymbals, ride cymbal, and two crash cymbals. Sizes vary considerably from 24"–18" bass drums, 8"–18" toms, and snare drums of all shapes and sizes. Drummers such as Louie Bellson, Keith Moon, Ginger Baker and Billy Cobham pioneered double bass drum techniques. Rock drummers at times used large tom and cymbal setups. As calfskin drumheads were replaced with plastic heads, a large variety of drum sticks and brushes were invented. Cymbals and gongs were made of different types of metals or alloys such as brass, copper, bronze, tin, nickel, and zinc.

Some drummers use triggers in their drumset and external pads to trigger samplers, loops, and other midi devices.

Listen to the drumset demonstrations on tracks 45 (A section), 48 (B section), 49 (Break in 7), and 51 (End Break). Then play along with tracks 53 and 54.

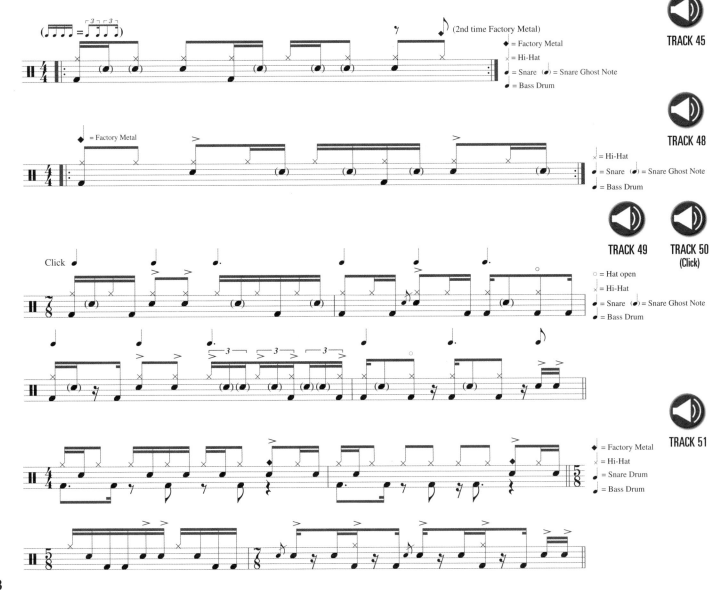

Tubano

Figure 1

Figure 2

The tubano, created by Remo, has a conga-like sound. They come in three different sizes (10", 12", and 14") and feature (key-tuned) NuSkyn heads that have a calf-like feel and sound. The traditional Cuban conga was made out of olive barrels or steamed bent staves of wood glued together. The heads were made of calf or buffalo skin and tacked to the wood. The tubano's innovative design features an internal resonating tube and cut-out feet to allow full bass resonance without using a floor stand or tilting the drum.

There is a broad range of sounds that can be produced depending on the hand position and where the drumhead is struck. One sound is the bass tone, the lowest frequency of the drum, which can be produced by hitting the center of the drumhead with the palm or fist. The open tones (see figure 1) can be achieved by playing with the fingers and palm towards the edge of the drumhead. The slap is a sharp defined sound, which can be played muted (see figure 2) or open.

Listen to the 12" tubano demonstration on track 46 (B sections) and then play along with track 52.

TRACK 46

○ = Open tones

Afuche-Cabasa

The Latin Percussion afuche-cabasa was developed by Martin Cohen and constructed using endless loops of a steel bead chain wrapped around a specially textured, stainless steel cylinder. The beads can be rotated around the textured steel, or the instrument can be spun or shaken for variety of sounds. The afuche-cabasa was designed to create rhythmic scraping sounds and patterns by holding the beads with one hand while the other hand holds the handle of the instrument to use a twisting back and forth motion.

Listen to the afuche-cabasa demonstrations on track 47 (B sections) and then play along with track 52.

TRACK 47

Hip Hop Chart

Now that you've learned the hip hop score and percussion break sections, listen to the entire composition on track 52 (with drums) and play along using the percussion instrument you've been working with. Then, learn a different instrument and play along with the ensemble.

When you are ready to play drumset with the composition, play along with track 53 (without drumset) or 54 (without drumset and drum loops).

TRACK 52
w/ drumset

TRACK 53
w/out drumset

TRACK 54
w/out drumset & loops

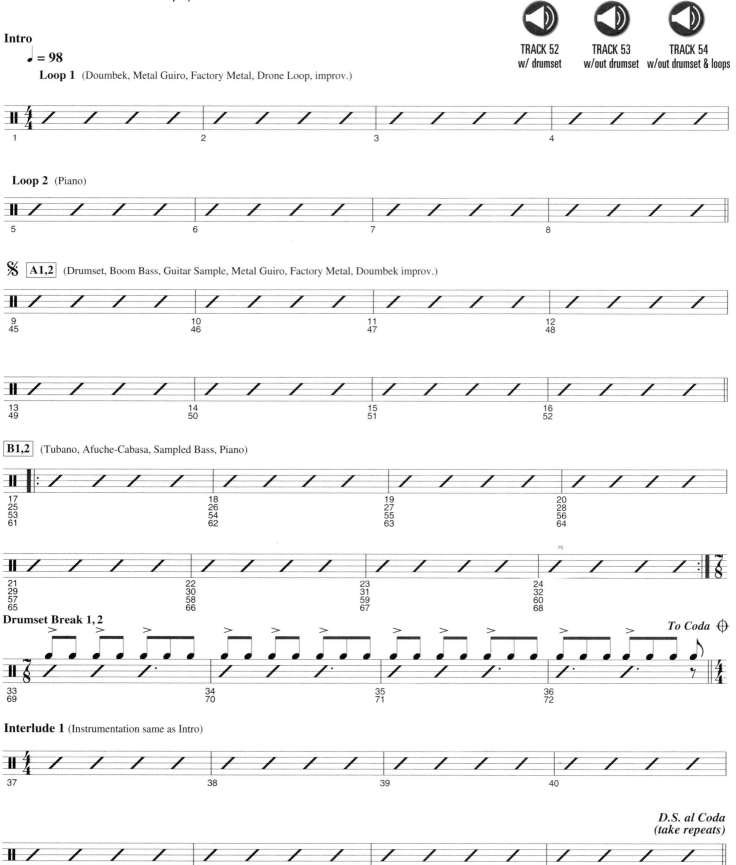

Intro

♩ = 98

Loop 1 (Doumbek, Metal Guiro, Factory Metal, Drone Loop, improv.)

Loop 2 (Piano)

A1,2 (Drumset, Boom Bass, Guitar Sample, Metal Guiro, Factory Metal, Doumbek improv.)

B1,2 (Tubano, Afuche-Cabasa, Sampled Bass, Piano)

Drumset Break 1, 2

To Coda ⊕

Interlude 1 (Instrumentation same as Intro)

D.S. al Coda
(take repeats)

61

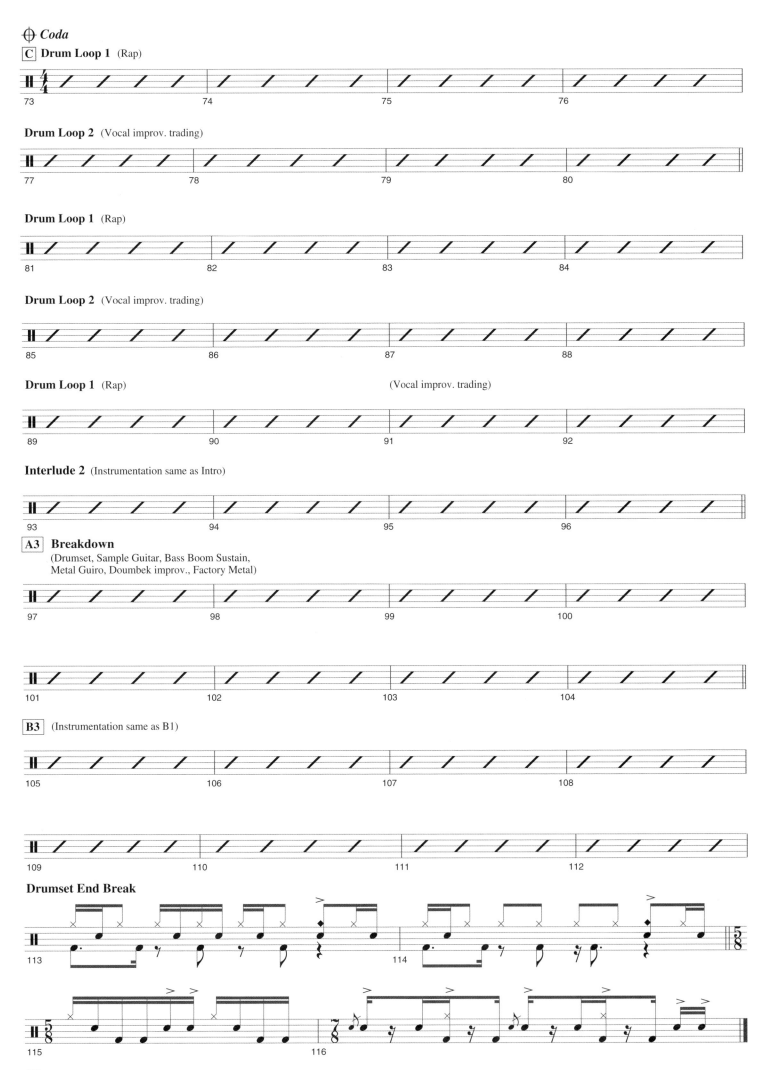

⊕ *Coda*

C **Drum Loop 1** (Rap)

Drum Loop 2 (Vocal improv. trading)

Drum Loop 1 (Rap)

Drum Loop 2 (Vocal improv. trading)

Drum Loop 1 (Rap)   (Vocal improv. trading)

Interlude 2 (Instrumentation same as Intro)

A3 **Breakdown**
(Drumset, Sample Guitar, Bass Boom Sustain,
Metal Guiro, Doumbek improv., Factory Metal)

B3 (Instrumentation same as B1)

Drumset End Break

Conclusion

In closing we would like to encourage you to focus on rhythmic awareness, time-feel, and self-expression through the language of rhythm. Good luck and keep groovin'.

Maria Martinez

Ed Roscetti

You can correspond with Maria and Ed and find out about their other publications, CDs, DVDs, videos, workshops, and clinics by visiting their websites at www.worldbeatrhythms.com and www.roscettimusic.com, or you can email them at workshops@worldbeatrhythms.com.